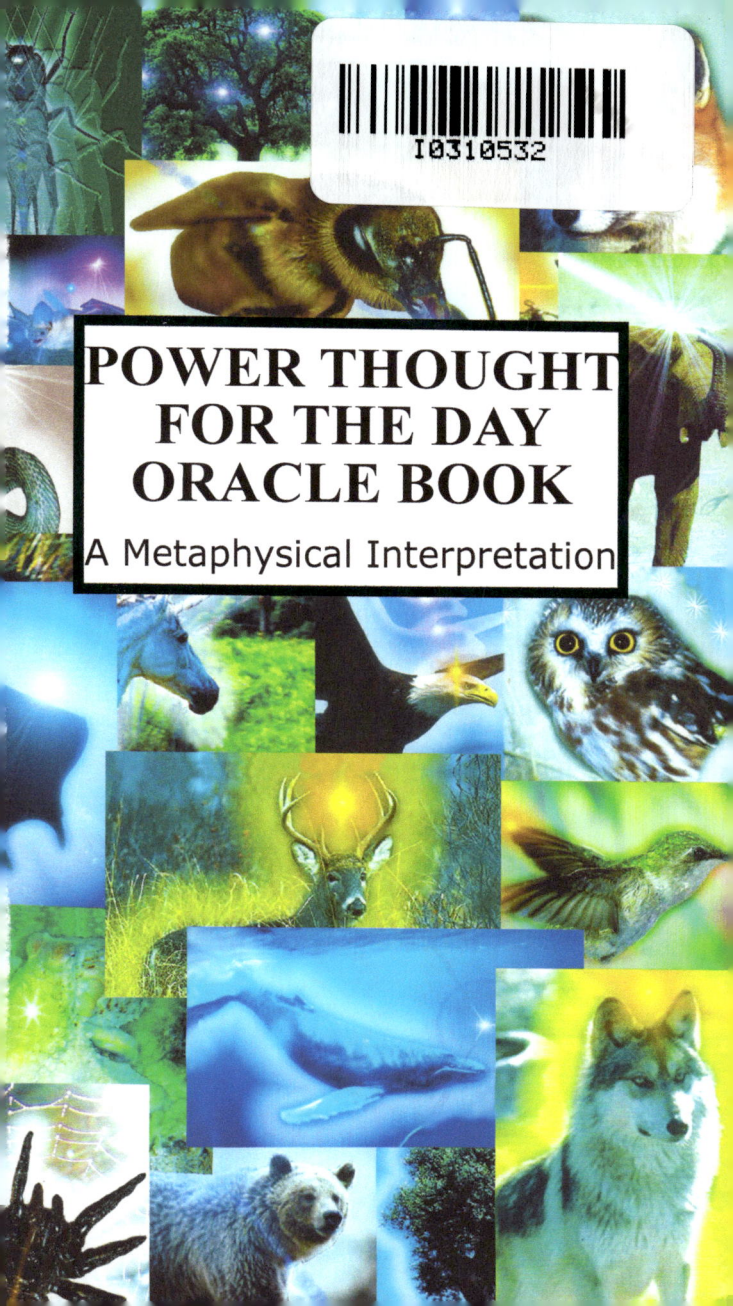

# POWER THOUGHT FOR THE DAY ORACLE BOOK

A Metaphysical Interpretation

# POWER THOUGHT FOR THE DAY
# ORACLE BOOK
# A metaphysical interpretation

## COPYRIGHT

Copyright © 2021 Margaret Ann Kelly (Omni)

All rights reserved. This book may not be reproduced, wholly or in part, or transmitted in any form whatsoever without written permission from the author, O.M. Kelly, www.elanea.com

The author of this book does not dispense medical advice or prescribe the use of any technique as a form of treatment for physical, emotional, or medical problems without the advice of a physician, either directly or indirectly. The intent of the author is only to offer information of a general nature to help you in your quest for emotional and spiritual well-being. In the event you use any of the information in this book for yourself, which is your constitutional right, the author assumes no responsibility for your actions.

## AUTHOR

Author O.M. Kelly, known as Omni to her clients and students is an internationally acclaimed author and lecturer, on Metaphysics, Philosophy and understanding the Collective Consciousness. Omni consults for Member States of the European Commission and other International Companies throughout Europe. Omni now resides on Australia's beautiful Gold Coast, writing books, and works as a Life Mentor and Business Coach. Omni's cumulative years of personal research and dedication to her journey, has lead to discoveries and initiations into the mathematical language of the unconscious mind (higher mind), all compiled into a nine volume masterpiece, 'Decoding the Mind of God'.

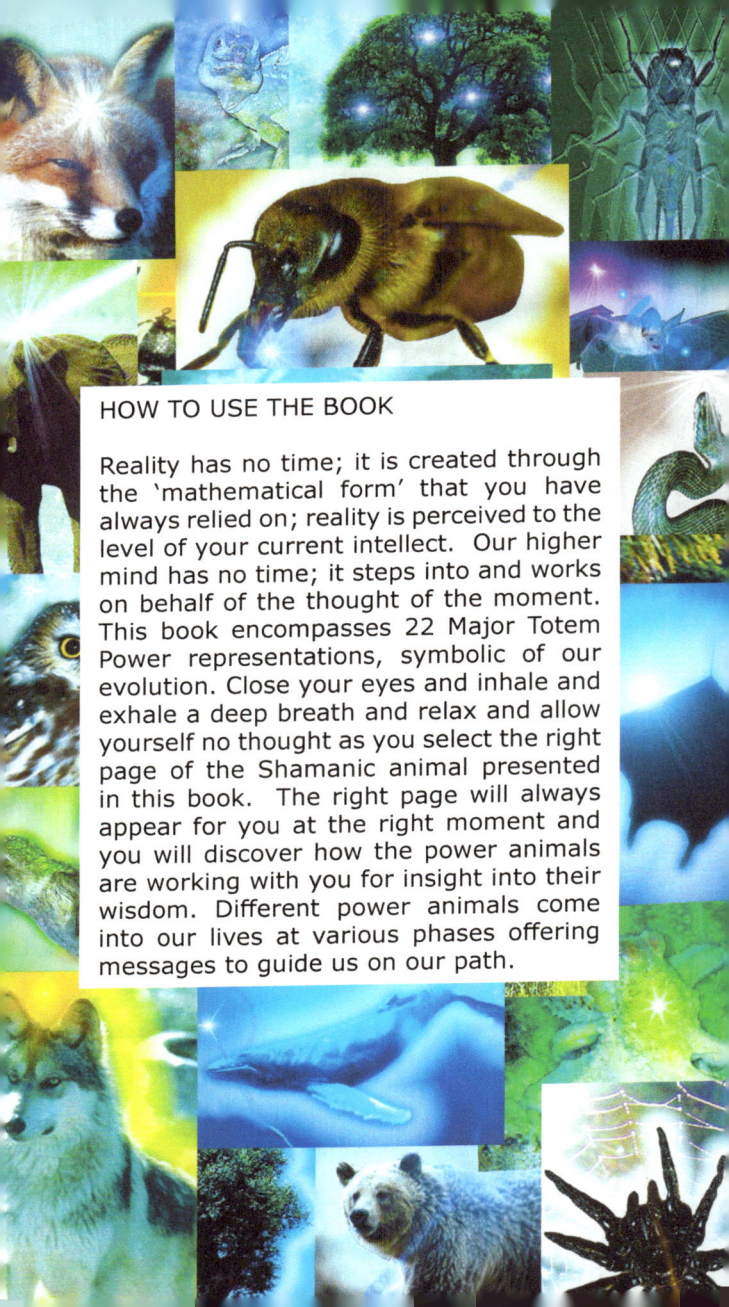

## HOW TO USE THE BOOK

Reality has no time; it is created through the 'mathematical form' that you have always relied on; reality is perceived to the level of your current intellect. Our higher mind has no time; it steps into and works on behalf of the thought of the moment. This book encompasses 22 Major Totem Power representations, symbolic of our evolution. Close your eyes and inhale and exhale a deep breath and relax and allow yourself no thought as you select the right page of the Shamanic animal presented in this book. The right page will always appear for you at the right moment and you will discover how the power animals are working with you for insight into their wisdom. Different power animals come into our lives at various phases offering messages to guide us on our path.

magnify holographically and lead the way for us to offer greater expectations to self.

Each step of evolution is opening us up to extra responsibilities of self and as we move forward we must accept the reasoning as to why they evolved in the first place. For you to progress in your mind, the old thoughts that you have hung onto for security must automatically release and diminish. The old story is repeatedly handed down to us with each generation. We must overtake the past generation knowledge and gain mastery of our own divine wisdom; otherwise the story is repeatedly creating the same mistakes over and over again.

We are now aware that the extinction of the Animal Kingdom could easily be an effect of human cause. We have overtaken their reasoning as to how and why they evolved in the first place. They now form the make-up of our second dimensional mind. We, as humans, must now accept our responsibility for the evolution of our animal species.

The dimensions presented in this introduction are the four directions that release you from your DNA. Each direction: North, South, East and West, is an evolutionary step of advancement into your acceptance of the responsibility of realising the potentiality of the alchemy that you control with your brain.

Through the 'Totem' energy of all, the ancient species that we have evolved before us, represent an emotional inheritance that we can rely on to sustain our moment. They will become the beneficial advisers to help us with our own intelligence when our mind is in the field of doubt.

Insects rely on their sonar, as they do not eat matter; they remove and digest only the juices. They represent the alchemy that we produce in the brain; these are resonances that we collate through the two holes in the roof of our mouth.

Now let us hear the above story again on a metaphysical observation: As the tree grows, it moves up and throughout our system. The animal becomes our ego. The bird evolution lifts us up into our angelic nature through the opening of the heart, where we offer to return our favours to others.

Then we move deeper into the collective consciousness of the ocean and we enter into the worlds of our unconscious mind (higher mind). This section of the brain is much greater in matter and holds limitless opportunities to benefit our future. The more we accept our own future. The more we accept our own intellect; the more we add to what we can achieve. This is the fourth dimension appearing into our psyche and it presents the opportunity for us to accept responsibility for the consequences that are delivered back to us through our higher mind. This is the world of cause and effect.

We now enter into the next evolution of humanity as the human brain begins to reinvest in itself. The layers of the Pia Mater (the piousness of self), the Arachnoid (the gathering of the web we weave) and the Dura Mater (the durability of self) are the three membranes that cover both hemispheres of the brain and the spinal cord. These membranes thicken and strengthen this outer perimeter and through time these layers will

Kingdom, which is collected and gathered from the navel to the heart. We begin to earn the strength of our heart when we enter into this Kingdom, through entering into and opening up our right brain. These are the worlds of our emotions or our 'energy in motion'. We have evolved and grown through our  confidence, trusting and believing in itself.

From the heart we move up into the chest area to the throat, which creates the third section and this is the evolution of the ocean.  The species of the oceans help us to release the intelligence of the unconscious mind (higher mind), the hidden mind; the one that we cannot see. It silently works on our behalf showing us our flaws through the injustices that we return to ourselves; we receive these thoughts through our vision world. We began to recognise this when we conceived of the word 'imagination' which, in our innocence we refer to as our dreams.

From the throat or the base of the brain we enter into the unconscious mind (higher mind) and this is the world of the insect. The insect has evolved to reduce and replace the irritations to the exalted mind. From here we have the power to hone into the potentiality of our sonar or sonic sound, which is the design of the inner ear, to correct the 'mathematics'; of the conscious and subconscious minds which, when understood correctly, are the worlds of the extra-terrestrial.

# POWER THOUGHT FOR THE DAY
## ORACLE BOOK
### A metaphysical interpretation

*You are and have always been
the greatest gift to the earth.*

Each species that has evolved on this planet is recorded in our cellular memory. Our thinking began with the world of Trees, where we yearned to stand upright. In the form of the human body, the tree species are embedded in the feet and lower legs. The tree's opposite was attracted and became the

worm. The worm came out of the oceans of consciousness to invest in the ground where its strength grew through the importance of

self, and then it evolved into the serpent, where it took its place above the ground.

The Animal Kingdom then took its place in our evolution where we learned to understand ourselves, and this understanding became the collective of our left brain. We released our tail and our rudder disappeared; our sole responsibility was passed down to us in order for us to steer our own vessel in the direction that we wished to travel. The taller we stood the more our consciousness expanded towards the

heavens. This second collection of evolution is situated from the knees to the navel.

The next step up the evolutionary ladder presented itself to us through the Bird

1.     SERPENT—Awakening

*The serpent symbolically represents the introduction to the initiation of your inner quest. It is connected to the evolution of the left brain/hemisphere (consciousness—ego) and is the advanced edition of the worm. The difference is that the serpent has bone tissue which represents the vertebrate of your spine that house and protects your bone marrow, or the root system of your DNA. Bone tissue is the gathering of your inner strength which becomes your intelligence. We have named the awakening of this first seal, which is the initiation into self, the Kundalini. The Serpent is also a warning that there is something you have overlooked in your decision making process. You need to work your way back to the beginning in order to find that missing link.*

Symbolically the serpent represents the unfolding of the twelve strands of your DNA and this can only be achieved through the yearning of both the left and right brains to harmonize and balance with one another. Learn to silence the chattering of your mind to such an extent that it could be said of you that you are living a 'walking meditation'. Meditation is the inner medication by which you can achieve 'all' by yourself, once you have attained the confidence to keep your mind in the silence it deserves.

Further explanation of the Kundalini—or the DNA unfolding—through the Tibetan and Indian law; it is the Feathered Serpent through the Mayan law; it is the Pharaoh of the Egyptian principles, with the two symbols of the serpent and the vulture.

## 2. LIZARD—The Devil's Advocate

*Allow this advocate to show you its strengths, not its weaknesses. If you select this page, Lizard is telling you to stop re-running the same old scene of repetitious thought. You are going nowhere, so move on.*

Lizard is known as the 'Devil's Advocate'. Lizard lives in the left brain/hemisphere (consciousness—ego) and will create many excuses through its controlling influence of refusing to understand itself. It (ego) requires your direct attention, where you have to be aware of how quickly your mind can search for an excuse to overcome your moment. Lizard is the serpent with legs, which runs over its territory and is afraid to step out of its own boundaries. It has created its own comfort zone through re-running the same thoughts over and over again. Metaphysically its cold bloodedness allows no emotions, and yet when balanced through reaching up to the right brain/hemisphere (subconscious-emotions), it has the potential to release a strength that lays untapped within.

When you feel trapped in an emotional situation that is not adding up; lizard has to accept the next responsibility of its current value (thinking), which is to bring you out of your reverie in order for you to become more focused on your intention. How to stop re-running the same old scene of repetitious thought? If that same memorial experience or thought is created back into your thinking again, you must stop it before it becomes greater. Try to search beyond the moment to see how this energy or thought re-created itself.

3. OAK TREE—Wisdom

*The Oak Tree is reminding you to weigh up the decision of the moment. Do not throw everything out. Stop choking your own light. Let your new ideas create their own shadows. Sit under your Oak Tree and reach for the acorns as they represent the progressive nature of your next thought.*

The Oak Tree stands for wisdom and is the elder to the tribe. Through all kinds of weather, the strength of its roots and trunk do not waver in the winds. Through the winter months the Oak Tree hangs onto many of its old leaves and those leaves represent the pages of our DNA, our inner library. It never lets go of the past until the new leaf, which has evolved the strength to create its own shadow, emerges.

We need this balanced growth to enable us to rest our minds in times of doubt. This solid tree helps to create the inner strength that we need to present our thoughts into our pituitary gland. This gland twists and moves through the storms we create in our mind. It has the responsibility of our intuition, to equate each of our thoughts and process them into either the left or right hemisphere of the brain before they settle into the memory banks. The wisdom you have learned on your life's journey up to this point is perfect for you; the next step on your life's quest is for you to understand yourself. You will ascend into a higher knowing of how you can live out your own intelligence. Every type of tree is unique in what it represents. The giant redwood represents strength. The apple tree is a blessing for self.

## 4. OLIVE TREE—The Mind

*If you have selected this page of the Olive Tree, you are urged by your higher mind to abstain from doubt. 'Lose self-doubt' when reversed becomes 'Doubt self and you lose'. Release the fear of your past and also the doubts that you have. Do not put your light out or dim the flame that keeps your heart alive. Release that inner strength; it is there in the wings, waiting to get to know you.*

More respect of self is needed in order for you to make further progress. Never doubt your endless possibilities.

The Olive Tree feeds the life force of the left brain/hemisphere (consciousness—ego). The tree in Shamanism is named 'Reproduction'. It never bears fruit in the same place twice, so pruning each year is a must. This tree has a life span of over 500 years and continues to bear fruit throughout its lifetime. This explains to us that the old thoughts cannot be used repeatedly; they must be pruned to allow new growth to appear. This is the tree that Solomon used in his Temple. It also represents the opening of the seventh seal of St. John in the book of Revelations. Once the seventh seal is opened, you are truly on your way to self-attainment. Every seven years a seed drops from the Olive Tree and travels underground into the base of that tree to replenish the original trunk. This new growth blends in with the old to sustain the life force of the tree. The result of the fruit is the oil it contains, which symbolically represents our pineal gland. This oil also symbolises the sanctification that we return to ourselves.

## 5. FOX—The Trickster

*If you have attracted Fox today, then become aware of the messages that you are giving out to others. They will think twice before they walk towards you and your expectations and you will come to realize that you are on your own. The more we deceive ourselves, the more the odour of the fox builds up in our body. People sense this energy when they walk into a room and so they know who to be more aware of and walk around.*

To create positive changes in your life, you must learn to accept a more advanced responsibility for self. Tree represents knowledge. Fox lives in amongst the roots of the tree so it means that he has all of his knowledge above him. He does not want to look up, therefore he has difficulties in acknowledging and seeing what is above him; he does not want to face up to his own responsibilities. He confuses himself and reaches out for his own satisfaction through sustenance from others. Fox's cunningness gets him out of unnecessary situations through his own demeaning of self. Your quest on this journey regarding earning the inner secrets of your life is a quest of you discovering and understanding the value of you; to place a value on yourself means that you are searching for the importance of your worth. You learn to respect yourself through the feelings of your own values accomplishing their own results, which support you, and you learn to stand taller as you walk through your genetic inheritance. Your life program keeps on creating itself through each of your thoughts building upon the other, and the transformation continues.

6.     BEAR—Serenity

*Selecting Bear is the message that there is no need to hurry. Take your time with important matters and allow each situation to quietly present itself to you. Bear walks alone and subjects are thoroughly thought out and digested before decisions are made, so stop chasing your own tail.*

When you feel harmonized within, you balance each decision with a new found serenity that helps you come to terms with each situation in the moment. Align yourself with quietness and think things through thoroughly before you act. If the important matters are concerning work, go back over your work as there is something else to gain from all of your endeavours, through you reaching a greater understanding of things. You must be clear in the mind, through creating a serene attitude over all thoughts, in order for you to be able to release and hear every aspect concerning the subject at hand. Salt from the roe of the salmon and sugar from the wild honey are the bears staple diets.  Salt and sugar also correlate and balance the alchemy of our mind.

Bear has no need for an ego; therefore he becomes the healer for your own self-esteem. He has control of himself and therefore can steer himself in any direction he chooses. What and how you are thinking right now is the result of what you have become; what you are doing on this journey of life is also learning to understand where you have come from. The abilities and opportunities you have understood so far will determine where you can go on to complete your journey of self.

7. WOLF—Focus

*Wolf's intention is one of pure power of focus. Wolf represents the 'Ancient Loyalty to Self'. Wolf's intention is through his own purpose to focus through his inner strength; nothing interferes with that focus. Through you selecting for yourself this page, you can see how this story relates to you; how you can accomplish the task at hand. You need to find the 'loyalty' that wolf has retained for you, to focus and keep all your energy aligned on the job at hand or inner direction you are taking.*

Stop your thoughts from chattering on unnecessary ideas. From an inner level, what we refer to as 'focusing' is like adjusting the lens on a camera; you receive a clearer picture by refocusing that lens. Learn to focus your mind and live permanently in the moment. If you are not focused in the moment and the mind wanders, just stop, reset, and say to yourself "now focus on the moment".

Wolf likes to work with the pack, not against it. He represents the pathways of our evolution, which is the belief in the knowledge that we have gained so far, through those who have walked before us. We all need our own loyalty to sustain ourselves with; this is the confidence that we achieve through our belief in self. We have named wolf, through the gift of Shamanism, the 'Inner Teacher'. He is the one who still holds the old codes that we have the ability to endow ourselves with. These codes are the sustenance that we feed to our ego, to create our possibilities to remain focused on what we are to achieve.

## 8. HORSE—Inner strength

*Selecting this page means that as you collect and bring together your thoughts today, they will be empowered by your deep desire for strength. Through the Laws of Shamanism, the Horse represents your 'Inner Strength'. We have fettered this animal to apply to our mental needs, as it has the extra strength that we require for the achievement of self. Horse carries and supports us and we ride on the currents of his expression to accomplish what we ourselves cannot do.*

Inner strength is an asset that you gather through the understanding and acceptance of your actions. It solidifies and strengthens your attitude towards yourself, and then in turn, towards others. When we bring the energy of Horse up into the mathematics of the mind (the energy of our thoughts), we find that the page you have selected today comes from the wisdom, or the wise domain, which you gain through the worlds of mythology. We have named this animal the Unicorn. We use this energy through the announcement of the third eye, which has been opened through finding our inner strength. Your inner strength is your expectations abiding in you. This happens when you understand and accept every experience of your life. Know how to build your own energy, as that is how your Law of Self—your own Universal Law—works for you. Listen to yourself, and then understand how others listen to you. Understand the importance of allowing your freedom to be free, to allow the motivation of the next thought to automatically come from the previous thought.

## 9. ELEPHANT—Knowledge

*Through the Laws of Shamanism, Elephant represents 'Knowledge'; as applied to the knowing of the ways. Elephant gifts you the message of knowledge, so use the power of your own mind. Elephant is the Pharaoh of the animal species, and as the largest of the land species enters into the 'Royal Behaviour of Self'. A further message today is to remind you of the respect for self.*

Keep your mind as pliable and as available as you can so that you have the ability to see 'over' all situations, taking them in your stride with ease. Metaphysically the gift that elephant gives us is that when Elephant calls to the tribe he/she can communicate to every other elephant on the planet at the same time. The vibration of the elephant's call is measured mathematically to resonate at around 2 megahertz. This collective tone (frequency of sound) that Elephant produces has the ability to travel along the ground without being disturbed by other species. Through elephants respect to self, his/her thoughts are able to echo along the earth plane and resonate through to the rest of the elephant species, combining telepathically with them so they actually strengthen the deed of the call.

Humanity still has the pleasure to earn (to achieve) elephants' vast intelligence. We still have a long way to go before we can equal the knowledge of their learned endowment. We must earn their wisdom. We have, within our DNA coding, the energies of all the creatures on the earth, and so we become their mirrors.

## 10. STAG—The Shaman

*You will need all of your inner strength and attention to see this day through. If you have chosen this page, something is about to happen which must reach fruition in your mind. The Golden Stag is available to assist you with your final decision.*

When Stag enters your vision world, you are being tested to carry the responsibilities you have earned. You are up in your own 'Royal Chambers' now. It is from here that you will learn to live in your 'Palace of Worthiness', so don't' lose sight of what you have set out to achieve.

The Golden Stag is the last and highest vibration in the Animal Kingdom. It is through the Laws of Shamanism that once all of your doors are open, through the yearning for self and the learning through self, Stag enters into the worlds of your earnings. He is known as the 'Protector of your Royal House'. Your royal house is the ultimate earning of the crown that you wear, and your crown is the gathering of your gems. These gems have fostered and created themselves through the vibration of your light, or intellect conforming judicially through the expansion of your thoughts. The more appropriate our knowledge the more our wisdom conforms to the justice that we so richly deserve. Stag has the answers for all concerned, as he has the antlers which have the ability to search the cosmos for the solution to any difficult situation that may come our way. He treads softly and lightly and never becomes bogged down with what is not relevant to this moment.

## 11. OWL—Retreat

*Strengthen your ideas and let the power of your thoughts be your own inner knowing. Allow yourself the time to know when the right moment appears. Your ideas are too open and are prancing around outside their own personal boundaries, so the wisdom of Owl asks you to retreat back into your inner circle.*

Draw in a deep breath through your nose, hold it without any pressure, and then slowly release the breath back into the consciousness, repeating the process until you feel the roll of your inner circle. This process helps concentration and focusing.

Owl is connected to the four directions of the night, North, South, East and West. Owl has x-ray vision and is able to detect the slightest disturbance through the visibility of vibration, which occurs through the third eye. This improves the eyesight of Owl to achieve a three dimensionally view of the world at all times. You have selected this page of Owl to remind you to bring all your senses together, in order to see and feel all aspects of self and what has been presented to you or will be presented to you. The page of Owl also represents the entering up into the angelic realms; relating to the emotional responsibility of our heart, learning to balance our thinking through the harmonizing of, and the mastering of, self. With the mastering of self the world awaits your intention. With focused thoughts, bringing them back into their own respectful state of grace, you can achieve what you are setting out to accomplish.

## 12. EAGLE—Vision

*The highest of all comes down to work with you today. Sitting comfortably on your left shoulder, Eagle makes you taller than anyone else who may cross your path. You are being asked to reach beyond and look through, not at, any situation that presents itself to you.*

The higher mind answers us metaphorically, where we learn to look through in order to see all things; we are no longer just looking at. Eagle represents the highest levels of the Laws of the Universe. Its nest is placed on the highest peak of the mountains and this allows its peripheral vision to extend far and wide. Eagle finds its resonance through riding the thermal waves of the earthly heavens in a circular motion, where his/her mind is always centered and still.

When Eagle flies across your path, hold and rebalance your momentary thought. The centered mind inherits the heights of the universe, where your vision of all things becomes clearer and you have the opportunity to search beyond the immediate horizon to extend your moment. Furthermore, when Eagle flies in a circle above us it creates an autonomic response in our nervous system, which pulls and lifts us up into a higher realm of our higher mind. Eagle acts on our behalf, his/her spiral creating an uplifting response in our DNA. Eagle helps you to ride the thermals of your own intellect. Your wings are outstretched and this gives you a greater opportunity to glide through your day. Allow your thoughts to soar and be picked up and carried with the wind.

## 13. HUMMINGBIRD—Resonance

*If you have selected the page of Hummingbird then become aware that when you are bogged down in any situation, you should keep you mind focused and in the moment. Hummingbird is an instant thinker and teaches us to gather our own light, or intellect, in order to lift up and carry ourselves out of any situation.*

Hummingbird multiplies its energy to such an extent that while flying it completes its task in seconds, not minutes. Through its swiftness, the collective consciousness attracts itself to the energy the Hummingbird creates; therefore it lives in perpetual energy in motion. It is known through the Laws of Shamanism as the 'Carrier of the Web of Consciousness'.

Hummingbird is a complete miracle that can create up to 40 strokes of its wings in a single second. Its colour creates its own luminous light through the arching of its responsibilities, which also creates a humming sound that is automatically attracted to our higher mind. It lives on the essence of flowers, which is the ultimate code of angelic resonance at this time in our evolution.

The hummingbird makes its nest by combining its own spittle with spider webs, which both come into the divine equation of self. Both are extremely strong and can withstand hurricane force winds without disturbance. This tiny bird lives in the rainforests of the planet as it needs those atmospheric conditions in order to absorb the moisture that it requires to sustain its own life force.

## 14. OCTOPUS—Action

*When Octopus enters your life the message is clear that you have not emotionally responded to a problem at hand in a way that will balance your thoughts.*

Your ideas are on the outside and reliant on others attention. Where is your dichotomy? The dichotomy of our thinking, where we bring our mind together and realize a foundation for ourselves in order to understand what we have already accomplished through our lived experiences. Allow your antennae to lift you up into a higher vibration in order for you to rearrange your thinking and receive a clearer answer to the problem. We release our antennae through our intellectual light's stimulation of our feelings, which tunes us into our higher mind.

Octopus represents action and is the first of the Royal Masters of the ocean to present itself. Its eight tentacles represent the action of our arms, there are two layers of suction cups on each tentacle. There is a new species of Octopus emerging which, as they evolve their species higher up into the collective consciousness, has released these cups and replaced them with antennae to collect more information. This brings the energy of the new species up and into the pyramidal section of our brain and this new evolution is a similar process to how our brainwaves multiply through the divine energy; which is through the gift that we return back to self. Octopus represents the progress and prosperity of all things. It is a master of disguise and can very quickly blend into any situation of its own proprietary earnings.

## 15. DOLPHIN—Fee Will

*You have chosen Dolphin as the Collective Consciousness has an important direction for you to follow throughout today. Allow your thoughts to become free from entanglement, and watch as you release the power to collect a greater substance to your knowledge, which will create new skills that you can tap into and benefit from. A focused mind can create on your behalf.*

Dolphin is the teenager of consciousness; the young warrior who is out there to win in any situation and who requires a harmonious mind in order to do so. They can empower their energy to suit any situation by opening themselves up to attracting the collective inheritance.

You have the ability to apply your energy at the same speed as others who are in your presence. When a Dolphin swims beside a fast-moving ship, the Dolphin uses the power—or the energy—of that ship to add to its own energy in order to propel its motivational expertise through the water. That also explains to us the understanding of free will. The thrust, which comes through the belief of its own empowerment, can keep the Dolphin's speed equal to the speed of the ship, where the Dolphin then has the opportunity to power beyond the ship, through surging into its own free domain—if it so chooses. It is as if an astral restaurant is supplying the Dolphin with nourishment from that energy. Free will is the teenager, and it is also the warrior earning his wisdom through achieving his own self-will.

## 16. WHALE — Conversation and Communication

*Whales represent the intelligence of conversation and communication. When Whale enters your life the message is to keep your thoughts clear and precise, as they resonate unconsciously to all who surround you. Remember you are solely responsible for everything you say and do. Choose your words eloquently and Whale will support you in communicating clearly.*

The Whale, in Shamanism, is the evolution of the word 'communication'. It represents the conversation, pulse, and tone throughout the Collective Consciousness, and it sends and receives sound only through that sonic level. The Whale's Spiritual awareness becomes the 'essence' that pronounces its own intellectual energy back to itself. Whales create fields of light energy that can be seen from great distances, even from satellites. That vibration collects, and then it is forced through the next field of energy until it completes a full circuit. Whales can hear each other's thoughts through the sonic sound that they produce, through the beat of their own heart. The whale can communicate to every other whale in the ocean at the same time. Their sonic sound waves are carried throughout the Collective Consciousness and lived by its entire species simultaneously. Their sound waves are collected and carried along the ocean floor. All species that vibrate to the same frequency can hear and understand this sonic sound. Whales live totally on the vibrations of the higher mind. This is the highest format of the mind, which we refer to as the 'Royal Behaviour of Self'.

## 17. MANTA RAY—The Oracle

*If you have selected this page of the Manta Ray then know that you are reaching a pinnacle in your life or your career. Stop being indecisive with yourself and be proud of what you have already accomplished. Rebalance your mind. Manta Ray is watching over you; it is your next step into the light of your future intelligence.*

Manta Ray is the highest of the oceanic species, which vibrates to both the left and right brain. The Manta Ray represents the oracle of harmonic convergence of all the species of the ocean. Symbolically, the ocean represents the divinity that we earn through the Collective Consciousness. Once we are balanced and free, the oracle awaits our proprietary earnings and is automatically opened to serve us all.

As the Manta Ray flows through the ocean he/she acts in the likeness of the 'Government Overlord' and as such, is available to be in the right position at the right time. Manta Ray does not step outside his/her own boundary and is always in balance with his/her mind. Manta Ray lives in the centre of the ocean and uses the equatorial energy to hone in on. Manta Ray harmonizes and gathers all information on appropriate matters through serving oneself, and is continually checking and cross checking that all things are running smoothly. Manta Ray swims just below the surface of the water; therefore he/she is in charge of every situation and is continually inspecting and respecting each scene that is presented. As a consequence, Manta Ray will succeed in all aspects.

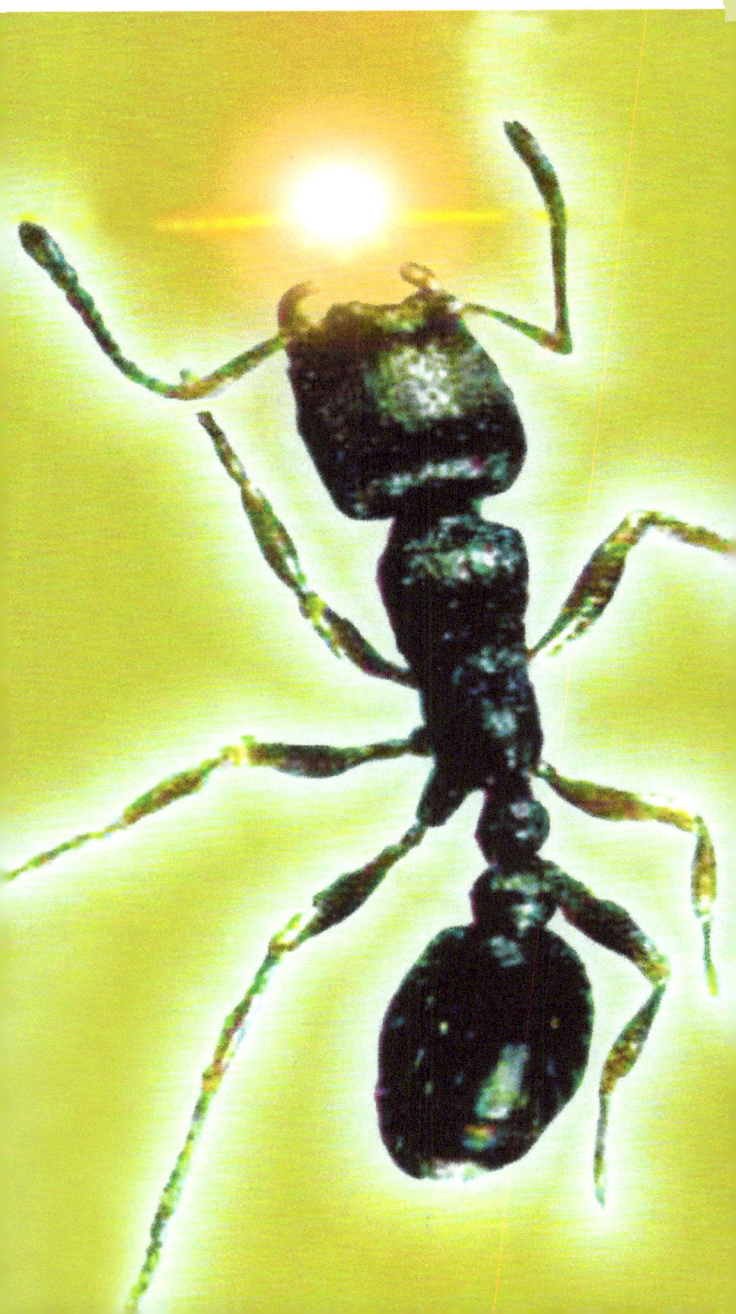

## 18.  ANT—Work

*You have now entered up into the sacred evolution of self through the Insect Kingdom. You are on the first step to entering up into your higher mind. It predicts hard work ahead of you so stop using excuses for your own repetitious performance. Learn to read the energy of what you have already accomplished and allow your senses the freedom to express a desire to move forward.*

Place your thoughts in alignment and finish the first thought before you move up into the next. Watch as your day multiplies, so that at the end of the day you will be amazed at what you have accomplished and achieved.

All insects represent the higher mind. The ant species have the largest brain of the insect world, and therefore have the opportunity to enhance their memory just like the whale an elephant do.

Ant has huge eyes just like the fly, which form a holographic view of seeing everything in a multiplied form. This holographic view gives them the benefit of reading the combustible energy that is released from food and is then registered through their antennae, which are their sensory glands. They receive and transmit responses of energy from a distance. Ant can lift twenty times its own weight, so responsibility for self is a must. An ant does not eat solid food; it squeezes the fluid out, drinks the life force and then throws the rest away. That nectar rearranges its alchemy immediately allowing it to open itself up to achieve more of its own cellular memory of its DNA.

## 19. BEE—The Gift

*Bee is extremely powerful. When Bee enters your life it means an end to ordinary things, as Bee signals the doorway into the 'Royal Approach to Self'. Bring yourself up into your hierarchical truth where you become a glyph or symbol that creates its own sound, a sound that everyone can hear unconsciously. Once your insecurities have diminished the 'Nectar from the Gods' is yours.*

The Bee's sting is created from its collected alchemy, which can become a hindrance to others. Poison is released from the unconscious mind (higher mind) and rids the self of insecurities. Like Ant and Fly, Bee hones in on energy and collects only the essence of all things. Bee is an insect of pure mathematics, which conforms into the geometry in our lives. Symbolically this is one of the highest orders that we can achieve. Bee has the wisdom to create the 'Nectar from the Gods' and its honey is needed by all the insect population to harmonize and balance their own survival. Bee, in Shamanism, is adding to the evolution of all insects, where the mathematics is now changing into the algebraic and geometrical equations. For your individual evolution a transition of consciousness must transpire, and in this transition it is important for you to understand that you are the most important person on this planet. Your individual consciousness (your life force) resonates to all. Through balancing your mind, you uplift your emotions, you become not only more aware of your intelligence but also more emotionally aware. This emotional intelligence is a perpetual motion.

## 20. CRICKET—Vibration

*You are being reminded to empower your thoughts and lift them up into a greater degree, where you have the ability to enhance your ideas and to surge forward. Reflect on your thoughts as you have set yourself down in a comfort zone that is no longer applicable to your moment. Cricket is asking you about how you have prioritized your thoughts and action.*

The Cricket antennae are longer than its body; hence its sonar reaching out and being able to read the energy that is applicable to its moment. It lives totally in its sonar or higher mind, and releases its energy through the vibration of rubbing its front wings, or its 'action', together. The more important it feels, the higher its vibration is recorded into the future, for all to accept and hear its information as a pathway for their own future development. Your Soul's journey is through the vibrational energy that releases from your thoughts—whether that is positive or negative energy. This is your life force collecting your consciousness in order for you to understand, through your innocence, where you are yearning for information; you also have an inner urge to awaken every cell in your body. Your Soul is your 'hidden' intelligence. There are three stages to the birth of a Cricket. Firstly, the eggs are laid underground, where they can then live as grubs for years. The second stage as an insect minus its wings. The third stage is when the cricket reaches maturity and develops wings and achieves its own perfection. Every human has to reach a peak of his/her own perfection in order to be exalted.

## 21. SPIDER—The Weaver

*Spider reminds you today that every thought you think is of utmost importance. Do not hinder your own wisdom.*

The Spider relates to reimbursing back into the higher mind. The second membrane that holds our spinal column and brain together is called the arachnoid. It is a very fine mesh-like membrane and looks similar to a spider's web and its purpose is to filter the temperature of our thinking. Spider has eight eyes and can see in all directions at the same time and also eight legs that have the understanding to walk in any direction at any moment of time. Spider is similarly related to the Octopus, which has eight arms representing 'action'.

Let the memory of what you have learned/earned in life, stand to attention and be available for you at all times. As stated above; do not hinder your wisdom. Wisdom can create the opportunity for you to dance with the Laws of the Universe. Your Spirituality is your essence; it is your energy formulating your wisdom. The Quantum Hologram that is the creation of all of us is comprised of these electromagnetic waves that cohere until they become coherent, and then they reform themselves. The higher and more powerful your vibrations become through accepting your intelligence and wisdom, the more your energy waves transforms into your Etheric Web—that is, the web of your Divine Consciousness, which is spread permanently out there, repeating itself throughout the Collective Consciousness, forevermore.

## 22. BAT—Sonar

*If you have selected this page today, then come into your silence and hone in on the importance of your words before you speak. Listen to your thoughts and always remember that the first thought is the right thought; it comes from your intuition, which is the inner teacher. Motivate your mind to see the whole outcome of a situation of what you wish to accomplish, before you begin to place your plans into action.*

The Bat is the 'Master' at work and is our introduction to our own sonic sound; which is the 'Production Company' of the higher mind. (Sonic sound: When we raise the level of our thinking and therefore vibration, this is when we harmonize our thoughts with the potential of 'the all' the unseen where the level of our thought creates and manifests into physical reality, matching the experience). The Bat has the responsibility of producing, through its own evolution, the unfolding of how we can birth our sonic sound, which allows us to speak what we have created from within. This is an introduction that takes us back into the ancient wisdom of evolution.

You have been given the ultimate doorway into the Law of Attraction to receive a 'repetitious' performance, that of your ideas being delivered back to you. Bat is the species that the Pharaoh Tutankhamen and Quetzalcoatl had placed over their mouths after death. The Bat has evolved through and released the feathers of the angel's wings. Revere the Bat because of what it has already attained. It has control over sight, hearing knowledge and brain.

www.ingramcontent.com/pod-product-compliance
Lightning Source LLC
Chambersburg PA
CBHW042349300426
44109CB00034B/30